Some Things Assistant Principals Do

Compiled by
Robert J. Kealey, Ed.D.

Department of Elementary Schools
National Catholic Educational Association

Copyright 2002
National Catholic Educational Association
1077 30th St., NW, Suite 100
Washington, D.C. 20007-3852
ISBN: 1-55833-286-3

All rights reserved, including the right of reproduction in whole or part in any form. Published in the United States of America by the National Catholic Educational Association.

Table of Contents

v   Preface

1   **Dottie Bessares**
       Young Author's Day: Student Authoring and Illustration

5   **Maria C. Carreras**
       Discipline, Love, and Learning

9   **Cindy Compagnone**
       Early Childhood Programs

13   **Suzanne Cowdrey**
       Virtue-A-Month Program

15   **Judith O. Fisher**
       Analyzing the Role of Disciplinarian

21   **Betsy Kingsbury**
       APEX – A Middle School Exploratory Program

25   **Stella Lauerman**
       Dual Roles

29   **Carolyn Levet**
       Growth for a Better You

33   **Sue Long**
       Science Fairs: A Valuable Tool in Mission Realization

39 Maureen Marsteller
A Plan for Local Inservice: Maximizing the Potential of Students Through Teacher Education

43 Jane Maurer
Fostering Responsibility and Accountability: B.I.S.T.

47 Amy L. Mead
STOP: Moral Decision-Making in the Upper Elementary Grades

53 Monica Moss
Safety in Our School

55 Mary Jean Quill
A.P.T. to Succeed

59 Carolyn Wilde
School Masses

Preface

The NCEA Department of Elementary Schools Executive Committee (DESEC) has taken the position that every Catholic elementary school should have an assistant principal. In most schools this position should be a full-time position. Over the past several years numerous new responsibilities have been bestowed upon the principal. The principal is expected to be the head teacher, curriculum developer, test coordinator, public relations person, development director, counselor, meeting attender, nurse, plant manager, and business manager, to name just a few. In addition the principal is charged with seeing that the students are receiving an excellent education and spiritual formation. No one person should be expected to fulfill all these roles. While many principals successfully delegate some of the above responsibilities to different members of the staff, some things can not be delegated and a person already doing a full-day of teaching cannot be expected to successfully carry out some of these duties.

The principal needs assistance and that is why assistant principals are needed. The principal and assistant principal should have clear job descriptions and know what exactly is expected of one another. While the principal remains the person in charge, some duties with the needed authority should be carried out by the assistant principal. Exactly what these duties are depends upon the talents and experiences of both the principal and assistant principal. Some principals have asked NCEA to develop a job description for the assistant principal. At this time the NCEA Department of Elementary Schools Executive Committee is reluctant to do this because the position is evolving and each school offers a different set of circumstances.

This is the second book that the NCEA Department of Elementary Schools has published on the assistant principal in the last three years. The first book is entitled A Day in the Life of a Catholic Elementary/Middle School Assistant Principal. The fourteen essays in that book were written by the participants of the first assistant principals' academy that NCEA held in the summer of 1998.

In the current publication, *Some Things Assistant Principals Do*, the participants at the 2001 assistant principals' academy related one of their chief responsibilities during the year. These essays deal with a variety of topics, e.g., discipline, school masses, early childhood programs, and many others. This great variety reflects the fact that some assistant principals were part-time while others were full-time; some came from small schools, others from very large schools; some schools were located in rural areas, others in urban centers.

The NCEA Department of Elementary Schools offers this book to its membership in the hope that they will be inspired by these stories. The one mark that holds all these different stories together is the clear dedication of the people to the ministry of Catholic education and children. The stories also show the amount of time that assistant principals spend on these programs. Finally, the reader will perceive that the schools' programs are enriched because one person had responsibility for these programs.

The department thanks its editorial assistant, Janice Kraus, for her work in bringing this collection of essays to the membership. It also expresses gratitude to Beatriz Ruiz for her cover design and laying out the pages.

Feast of St. Joseph, Husband of Mary, 2002
Department of Elementary School
National Catholic Educational Association

Janet P. Murray, M.A.   *Robert J. Kealey, Ed.D.*
President   *Executive Director*

Young Author's Day Student Authoring & Illustration

DOTTIE BESSARES
Assistant Principal
Precious Blood School
Los Angeles, CA

"The ultimate goal of teaching is to produce students who can learn and think for themselves" ... "Learning is a journey - not a final destination" ... *"Nothing great was ever achieved without enthusiasm"* ...

Students do not keep their "A" tests or essays, but they do keep their own authored and illustrated books! We have an exciting event at Precious Blood School where we celebrate bookmaking projects (K-8). Parents are invited into our parish hall that evening to see our celebration of books. This is learning at its best!

The action-based teaching of these kinds of projects is beneficial. They teach organization, consistent study habits (plan your work and work your plan), creativity, writing skills (structure, grammar, punctuation, spelling, etc), and communication.

Authoring and illustrating books is effective, fun, and motivates the learner. I integrate book making in all curricula. Last year my 8th graders made 12 books each (from 14 pages to 38 pages).

We started with book activities that ignited their interest

and stimulated their curiosity and empathy. They were able to experience and interpret what they had learned in many ways. Bookmaking provided experiences that helped clarify their thinking, deepened their understanding of content, and helped them to realize new insights. It allows students to relate the work to their own interests, lives, and experience.

Some helpful hints in getting kids to write and illustrate books successfully include:

- start with journals and quick-write reflections;
- double-entry journals (include "open mind", "hot seat", "readers' theater" etc);
- poem rendering (creating found poems from stories, poems, etc);
- allowing a "variety" of books that are of high interest to children (fun to do —like flip books, reversible books, "O" ring books, spiraled books, shape books, accordion books, dimensional character books, pop-up books, step books, etc);
- always grade positively on "content" (praise them) and include a second grade to cover neatness, punctuation, grammar, spelling, etc.;
- include a last page ("Readers' Comments") where all of their peers will read and look at their books and write a positive sentence or two;
- set the tone for excellence immediately for making a well-made book (each book must have a copyright page, dedication page, and a title page). Some books have a contents page, a "meet the author" page (complete with their picture and a synopsis all about them, and a "My Thoughts" page (their final thoughts/reflections upon completing the book) reflection;
- Encourage the cover of the book to be dimensional (creative).

We set the goal at Precious Blood School that "Reading is

the key to ALL academic achievement." I myself encourage various reading challenges. At the two schools in which I have taught at we have challenged the students to read a certain number of books by a certain date; if they do, the principal then has to spend the day on the school roof. What great motivation for kids! The day the principal went on the roof was highlighted with balloons, a decorated bucket to let down to receive class cards, letters, and treats, the police coming by with sirens saying hello to the principal on the roof and congratulating students, local newspaper pictures and write ups, etc. This motivated us to transition to student authored and illustrated books, a "Young Authors' Evening" (to display for parents and community), and much more reading and writing going on at school and at home. It definitely helped each student become a user of knowledge and not just a consumer of facts. And oh – what it does to self-esteem and confidence!

Discipline, Love, and Learning

MARIA C. CARRERAS
Assistant Principal
St. Kevin Catholic School
Miami, FL

The mission of Saint Kevin Catholic School is to assist the parent, the prime teacher, in educating the child spiritually, intellectually, socially, emotionally, and physically to attain each individual's potential to successfully live the teachings of Christ. Although the mission states nothing about discipline, it is an integral part of being a good Catholic. This is the reason why discipline is deemed as a fundamental and essential part of the education program at Saint Kevin.

The students of Saint Kevin Catholic School are required to follow certain rules of discipline. Motivating the children to develop the right attitudes toward discipline and responsibility is inherent to the school's philosophy. It is just as essential to maintain an effective plan to prevent discipline problems, as it is to uphold policies and procedures to tackle discipline problems. The parents are made aware of the rules of the school and the consequences of not adhering to these rules. The *Student/Parent Handbook* clearly states the proper habits and attitudes which are consistent with our education philosophy and mission. It stresses the commitment to the development of love of God and neighbor, respect for yourself and others, and the virtues of truth, justice, and honesty that are constantly emphasized in the classroom.

Responsibility leads to self-discipline. The older the child, the more responsible he/she will be held for his/her actions. The teachers are responsible for the disciplinary measures in their classrooms. Since the school caters to children from Pre-kindergarten through eighth grade, the disciplinary procedures are separated into three different categories.

From a very young age children need to be taught the difference between what is right and wrong. A sense of right and wrong is easily enforced through the acceptance of good behavior and the rejection of wrongdoing. In the Early Childhood Program, students are rewarded for doing what is right and correct. At this age level most of the discipline is corrected by the discipline procedures that the teachers have created in their individual classrooms. However, if that system is not adequate or a more grievous action occurs, then the teachers use a Conduct Report. The teacher completes this form, detailing the incident. It is then sent home with the child and must come back signed by the parents. The teachers keep a copy and the administration saves the other.

In the intermediate grades, third through fifth, once again teachers follow different discipline tactics in their classrooms. If a child, however, is defiant or commits a more serious disruption then the teacher may send home a Disciplinary Action. This form explains the incident, the date a detention will be served, and the punishment, which must be completed by the next day. Once the form is signed by the student and the parent, the teacher keeps the original and a copy is sent to the administration. Detentions usually are enough to deter serious discipline problems in the intermediate grades.

The older students are held more responsible for their actions. The junior high is departmentalized and so it is important that there be a system that is consistent throughout. For this purpose, the teachers follow a Demerit System which is very comprehensive and methodical. Two types of consequences, Major or Minor Demerits, may be given for different incidents or the extent of an infraction. Demerits are written in duplicate.

The original is sent home for parent's signature and the teacher issuing the demerit retains a copy. The original is returned to the teacher the following day and he/she will send it to the Council Coordinator who administers the system.

The Minor Demerit is a detention which is served after school. A Major Demerit is given for a more severe breach. Minors are accumulated and once a child receives four it become a Major Demerit. When a child has a Major Demerit he/she must appear before the Council of Junior High Teachers. The council consists of all the junior high teachers and the assistant principal who serves as Council Coordinator. There the teachers confer with the student regarding his/her behavior and a proper method of discipline will be determined. The teachers counsel the student in order to prevent any further violations. If a child receives a second Major Demerit, the child once again attends Demerit Council but this time the parent must attend as well. After Council the child serves a total of six hours of detention after school. Demerits are accumulated for a single school year. All demerits are destroyed at the end of the school year. Demerits may jeopardize participation in extra curricular activities, field trips, and honor societies.

At the roots of these disciplinary procedures is a very strong religion program throughout the school. The Ten Commandments serve as the guidelines and backbone for the discipline structure of the school. Moreover, all students receive development guidance classes by the school's Guidance Counselor to learn life skills, conflict resolution strategies, anger management, self-esteem, motivation, attitudes behavior, and development of character.

As the mission states, the parent is the prime teacher. The parents, therefore, are asked to become a part of the child's educational formation by supporting the school and participating in school related activities. The school's rules and regulations are consistent with the Catholic faith. These develop in the students the basic truths of honesty, justice, sincerity, responsibility, loyalty, cooperation, concern for others, and recognition of authority. The parents recognize that the teacher takes the place of the parent while the child is in school. Through strict discipline the school provides a safe and secure environment where learning can take place as love and respect prevail in every classroom.

Early Childhood Programs

CINDY COMPAGNONE
Assistant Principal
St. Mary School
Salina, KS

The mission statement of our school says that:

We will educate the whole person—body, mind, and spirit—in Christian values in accordance with our Catholic faith tradition. We are committed to providing a value-based environment that is conducive to the individual's academic, spiritual, social, and physical growth.

As assistant principal, much of my time is given to our early childhood program. Strong attention to this program is essential for the overall success of the school. Many parents who enroll their children in our pre-kindergarten tend to "buy into the program" and continue in our school as they become involved in the school community.

A very important part of my job is visiting the early childhood classrooms frequently. As the evaluator of its teachers, I can get a better feel for how they are doing the more I visit. I also take the time to speak personally with the teachers about their evaluations.

I not only observe the teachers, I also seriously observe the students. Since this is the first school experience for most, it is important that parents be made aware of any concerns such as developmental delays or social concerns that exist in the classroom. After consulting with the teachers about their students, we agree upon any type of communication we must conduct with the parents. If necessary, it is my responsibility to find any special resources in order to help children with their needs.

Another way our school looks at individual students is through kindergarten screenings, held during the spring before students enter kindergarten. The extra time given for this has many benefits. The screening gives the early childhood teachers, as well as the parents, a total picture of their child. As assistant principal, I organize the screening itself, which includes getting materials ready, meeting with the screening team, and developing the schedule. Many times, after the screening is complete, more than a letter is necessary to report back the results to parents. Therefore, I meet with parents to discuss the screening until they feel comfortable making any decisions related to it.

Parents are a very important part of our school's mission. I have organized a parent volunteer program that includes a volunteer training session. Parents are informed of important issues such as professionalism, confidentiality, and their role in the classroom. At the end of the school year, I review an evaluation from both teachers and parents on the program itself in order to make any adjustments for the following year.

Communication with parents is extremely important, especially with those who have their first-born entering school. We choose two nights in the spring to devote to parent information nights for parents of pre-kindergarten and kindergarten students entering in the fall. The teachers of those students are also present to discuss the curriculum, schedule, supplies and more. My role is to add the overall tone to the meeting— the mission of our school. These meetings are scheduled only for parents.

At the pre-kindergarten or kindergarten round-up we also give prospective students the opportunity to visit the grade level that they will be part of. Once again, the details of scheduling become my responsibility. Students visit classrooms for forty-five minutes, enough time to relieve their anxieties about coming to school.

There are many special events during the school year that involve the entire early childhood team. The more we meet together and communicate, the stronger the early childhood program will be. During the busy school year, however, it is easier to go about the business of teaching than meeting. Therefore, I organize monthly meetings for the team not only to discuss upcoming events, but also items in the curriculum. For example, the kindergarten teachers should be aware of what the pre-kindergarten has already covered, so as not to repeat it. Other examples would be discussions of field trips or themes in the classroom.

There is also a day-care center on our campus. We have a director who is responsible for her own staff. I am considered the director's supervisor. The day care center has an enrollment of sixty students. Many of those students are at the day care before or after the half-day pre-kindergarten and kindergarten sessions. Again, it is important that the lines of communication are kept open between the day care and the school. I visit with the director almost on a daily basis, just to keep in contact with any new happenings.

The early childhood program in our school is almost a school within a school. The students in the program make up half of the entire school. I consider this role of my assistant principalship highly important. As our mission states, we are committed to providing a value-based environment for the individual. By working together with strong unity, I believe the early childhood team can make this happen.

Virtue-A-Month Program

SUZANNE COWDREY
Assistant Principal
St. Mary's School
Pinckney, MI

It is the mission of Saint Mary's Catholic School to be a partner with parents in the spiritual and academic education of their children. This Catholic education is rooted in the Gospel teachings of Jesus Christ and takes place in a joyful atmosphere where students are encouraged to achieve individual excellence both in living their faith and pursuing academic excellence.

In keeping with the mission statement I developed a Virtue-A-Month Program. In August, I submitted a list of virtues that would be highlighted each month during the school year. The list included: Friendliness, Honesty, Faithfulness, Responsibility, Cheerfulness, Acceptance, Hardworking, Generosity, and Citizenship.

On the first Tuesday of each month I presented the virtue for that month at the All School Morning Prayer. I always began with an example of Jesus and how He lived out the virtue in His daily life. A story or reading was taken from the New Testament that pointed to the concept. Then concrete examples were given as to how the students could live out the virtue. Teachers then returned to their classrooms and used the idea as part of their religion class for that day. The seventh-grade class made posters each month focusing on the virtue. These were laminated and hung in the school as a reminder.

Nomination slips were passed out each month to the teachers for their students to use. The slip would state:

_____has shown
(Name of Student)

_____ by
(Virtue)

_____
(Give a concrete example)

_____
(Signed)

Students, faculty, aides, and parents were encouraged to fill out a slip when they observed someone who was living out the virtue. A brightly colored decorated box was placed outside of the office for nominations.

The nominations were collected three times a week and the person's name that was nominated was printed on a star – a different color for each month. The stars were hung from the ceiling in the main hallway of the school, beginning by the prayer center and stretching to the upper and lower elementary portions of the building. A display was set up by the office, showing the virtue and the color of the star that represented it.

The students were always interested to see the new stars as they were hung up. Parents, teachers, aides, staff, parish members, and students were nominated. It was most interesting to read why people were nominated. It made all of us look at ourselves in a new way – how small acts of kindness can make such a difference in the lives of others. The hallway looked great and the stars were a constant reminder of our goal to live as Jesus did.

Analyzing the Role of Disciplinarian

JUDITH O. FISHER
Assistant Principal
All Saints Catholic School
Manassas, VA

Most people who hear that I am an assistant principal automatically think "disciplinarian." Of course, that is one role outlined in my job description, but it means much more than the word usually connotes. My role is to assist the principal in helping our students develop the morals and values of Catholic Christians. In taking on this task, I recognized that my previous experiences with discipline came from the viewpoint of a teacher dealing with middle school students and so it became clear that preparation for this new role was a must.

One of the first things I did was to study our mission statement to be certain I was firmly grounded in the fundamental principles of the school philosophy. I keep a copy of this statement on my desk, which I read in the morning before the school day starts. At our morning prayer circle I pray that every member of our school community grows closer to God each day. After sitting in on several parent conferences with the principal, I recognized that prayer at the beginning of the conference helps each participant to focus on the Christian, moral dimensions of the discussion. Once this tone is set, discussion usually becomes a creative problem-solving session with the student's character development as well as the welfare of the school community as the focus.

Then I did some refresher work in the field of child development, reviewing the attributes and behaviors characteristic of children at each level of development. As a parent I had had firsthand experience with these stages as my three children grew and matured. However, because of the institutional nature of schools, there are different behavioral expectations than in the home environment. Thus renewing my knowledge of what constitutes age-appropriate behavior for differing ages of children was helpful to me. I also took some time to review our school's *Parent/Student Handbook* with respect to behavioral guidelines as well as diocesan policies.

Students from kindergarten through eighth grade are referred for administrative intervention. If possible, I speak with the referring teacher before conferring with the student. Knowing ahead whether the behavior is chronic or a first-time incident, how the teacher has dealt with the student in the past, whether the student is experiencing any peripheral difficulties, etc., better prepares me to assist the student. When this is not possible, the conference with the student must bring these points out so that I can evaluate the situation.

Most students consider that a visit to a principal's office means that they will receive some type of punishment for their actions. Certainly, this is sometimes the case, but not always. Since the goal of discipline is to assist students in forming their consciences and subsequent actions according to the mind of Christ, there can be many outcomes of such meetings. For some students the very fact that they have made a mistake and are responsible for informing their parents about it is punishment enough. Some students in the upper levels of middle school may be approaching the point of conscience development in which punishment is almost never needed. What these students need is a frank discussion of the situation and an evaluation of the circumstances that led up to the problem. In this way the student can take the initiative in righting the situation and avoiding the same circumstances in the future. These students also need positive encouragement in developing their moral sense because it is difficult to make the transition from externally imposed punishment as a means of erasing one's guilt to assuming the burden of dealing with guilt responsibly on one's own.

Some students may act out because of something not even school-related that is bothering them. With appropriate guidance the student can learn how to deal with such situations without misbehaving. Occasionally, I may ask a student to check in with me briefly each day or once a week for a specified period of time so I can provide the needed encouragement. Regardless of the action I take with the student, it is important that the student understands, according to his ability to do so, that what he did that was wrong and the effect his action had on himself and others. Together then we can work out an action plan for future behavior.

When dealing with several students who have disrupted the learning environment together, I find it helpful after listening to each student to bring the members of the group to a common understanding of their responsibility. Depending on the age of the students, this may require the assignment of blame, but that is not the purpose of the conference. Several programs that have laid the groundwork in our school for getting a group to restore harmony are the Catholic Virtues Program and the practice of stewardship. Because the entire school works on the same virtues at the same time and practices stewardship year round, all the students relate to these concepts. Very often it is possible to help students discover the incongruity between their actions and the practices and principles of these programs. Although examples must be concrete and discussion very short for the younger students, older students can come to the understanding on their own and in many cases verbalize it well.

When punishment is necessary, I try to keep the development of the student in mind. Primary students do not usually make sound causal connections; likewise, their focus time is not long. Therefore, punishments should not be of excessive duration and should follow the misbehavior as soon as it is practical. Regardless of the students' ages it is important for them to be able to repair the damage they have caused. I try to find something that can be done by the students to achieve this purpose. Often I ask students what they are going to do to make restitution. This question prompts students to think through the effects their actions may have had on others and begins to develop in them the concept that punishment does not relieve them of the duty to try to mitigate or even reverse the ill effects of their actions.

Older students may be given time to write down a plan of action together. For example, one group of students who put their own plan together after pushing band stands and chairs all over the room as a "joke," decided they would come in every band day before school and set up the stands and chairs for class. They did this faithfully for the remaining months of the school year, earning the gratitude of the band director. I know that the service approach these boys took had a more positive effect than any punishment I could have assigned.

Creative solutions to behavior problems tend to be productive in the long term. Several girls of middle school age were often in trouble together for things they talked each other into doing. After one incident that was more serious than most, I informed them that we were going to work together after school for a week doing positive things. For the first three days they worked together doing services for the school. On the fourth and fifth afternoons I asked them to plan a party-type breakfast for the sixth grade patrol students. They designed invitations for each student, the teachers, and the principal, made "thank you" banners, and planned decorations. On the day of the breakfast, the students decorated the room, blew up balloons and provided music. It was the nicest brunch we have had to date, with both the sixth graders and the planning committee being very pleased. The discussion as the girls and I cleaned up afterward centered on doing things that are positive and helpful for others rather than doing negative things when they are together. It was a point well taken.

If I ask students to apologize in writing, I read the letters before they are given out to be certain they are presentable and send the proper message. Often I am amazed at how accurately students realize the pain they have caused another student and at the genuine tone of the apologies. I find that any glibness that might have come out in an oral apology is not usually present in a written one. Young students sometimes do not understand the meaning of saying they are sorry. They may feel that it's one of those "magic" phrases and it excuses anything they have done. So when I ask these students to apologize, I make certain they know that it means not only that they are sorry, but also that they will not repeat the action again.

After handling discipline situations, I am careful to follow up with the referring teachers so that they are aware of anything that came up during my discussion with the student that might be important for them to know, such as any consequences that may have resulted. If I think it is necessary to contact parents about a discipline situation, I also let the teacher know about that contact. Keeping parents informed about their children is important so that they can work together with the school for the student's improvement. I also make certain the principal is informed about disciplinary situations. Even if he does not become involved in the situation, he needs to know what has occurred and how it was brought to a conclusion so that he can speak with parents if they have any concerns.

I also assist the principal in situations concerning serious offenses outside of the norm. When faced with serious a situation, we discuss it and its possible ramifications and then I may do some initial fact-finding and sorting out with the students involved. This can be a real time-saver for the principal. Given this information, the principal then brings the matter to resolution with the students and their parents. Some misbehaviors fall under clearly stated policy guidelines whereas others are not as clear-cut. The principal and I often discuss these situations before the best course of action is decided upon. This is an important part of the Assistant Principal's role because it allows all aspects of the situation to be examined and the various consequences for the student and the school to be reviewed and clarified by more than one person.

Many things can work to make the tone of the school happy and positive for our students. This type of environment is probably the strongest factor for good behavior that we can cultivate. Other things that I find that proactively encourage the students include: learning students' names and using them, visiting the classrooms often, showing interest in students' activities and their work, being present at lunch and recess *very often*, being present when students are changing classes, and establishing a positive rapport with students. Times when it is more important than usual to be present around the school are the week before major holidays, during any prolonged period of bad weather necessitating indoor recess, and the last few weeks before summer vacation.

Although many people think only of the negative aspects of the disciplinarian's role, I truly view it as the area where I can make the most positive enduring difference in our students' lives.

APEX – A Middle School Exploratory Program

BETSY KINGSBURY
Assistant Principal
St. Charles Borromeo School
Orlando, FL

According to some of the latest research, the middle school years may be second in importance to the first two years of life in determining the future success of children. That is one reason I have devoted so much time and energy in developing and implementing St. Charles Borromeo School's middle school exploratory program, APEX (Activities and Programs for Enhancement and eXpansion). Middle school students are unique in that they are old enough to need to take on some responsibility for their own learning, but they do not really know who they are, where their talents lie, or even why they do some of the things they do. They live an emotional roller coaster, insecure and tentative one moment, but confident and assertive the next. APEX is an exploratory program that permits young people to investigate various areas of curriculum, from the arts to competitive academics, to explore their emotions and needs, and encourages them to make real choices that matter. APEX attempts to help middle schoolers discover what they like to do, what they are good at, who they are, and more importantly, what they could become.

Unlike wheel programs, in which all students rotate through the same few courses during the course of a year, APEX consists of over 180 different mini-courses in three major areas: Communications (including Foreign Language), Computer Applications, and Literature; Fine Arts, Physical Education and Health; and Core Curriculum Enhancement. All middle school teachers, all special area teachers, the guidance counselor, and even some parent and parish staff volunteers have become involved by creating and teaching these mini-courses. The courses are developed with the understanding that they need to be high interest, that they will be multi-grade, that the assessment is primarily performance based (and graded only Pass-Fail), and that they must be curriculum-based.

Because the courses have been created by those who will teach them, they draw on the interests and talents of the teachers, and the teachers take special pride in developing courses that will be popular as well as meaningful. The Middle School Bands and Choirs meet to practice during some of the APEX class periods, but since there are nine APEX periods each week, participating in those activities does not exclude students from trying other courses as well. Some of the more successful classes include Stained Glass Studio, Quilting, Rollercoaster!, The Theology of Star Wars, Community Service – What is it and Why?, and Musical Theater.

While the wide variety of exploratory classes provides high interest, the most valuable aspect of APEX, in my opinion, is that it permits students of widely varying abilities and levels of achievement to challenge themselves in a non-threatening environment. It also provides extra help in reading, composition, and mathematics if they need it. Students for whom core curriculum subjects come easily can read Shakespeare or Mark Twain, participate in competitive creative writing and essay contests, and enter mathematics challenges and competitions. Our school population is approximately 10% Hispanic, and many of our students come from bilingual homes, while other students arrive at middle school with almost no knowledge of Spanish or any other foreign language. During APEX, students can take the appropriate level of Spanish, ranging from the very basic introductory course to the more advanced Spanish for Bilinguals.

And students who arrive at middle school still lacking some basic skills can take remediation workshops in which their needs are determined, targeted, and met.

The Workshop classes are the only classes in which students are placed by teachers. Math Workshops meet once or twice each week and are designed to help each student discover and fill gaps in mathematics background skills. The mathematics teachers, along with an instructional assistant, pre-test students who are having difficulty in computation and then design individual programs for students to follow. Students who complete their programs are then exit-tested to be certain they have accomplished their goals. In addition to workshops, APEX also provides in-school mathematics help sessions in which the mathematics teachers are available to answer questions about regular math class material and provide help as needed.

Grammar and Composition Workshops help students who are having difficulty with the basic writing skills necessary to succeed in middle school. Students are encouraged to pre-write, write, critique, edit, and re-write paragraphs, short answers, and essays to prepare them for writing in their various content areas.

Reading Comprehension Workshops are so popular that even some students who are not recommended choose these classes. Each course focuses on a short novel. The novels are chosen for their appeal as well as their quality; among the more popular have been *To Kill a Mockingbird* and *The Watsons Go to Birmingham*. The students are assigned to read a chapter independently only after they discuss vocabulary, context, and the story line in class. After reading, the class then discusses each chapter, dramatizes parts of it, and even watches parts of videos to help students understand what the author has done and why. The teacher has consistently succeeded in teaching reading skills and encouraging independent reading by building confidence and interest.

The final component of the APEX program is the incorporation of a weekly Advisory class. During Advisory students participate with other members of their homeroom classes in activities that build community. Older students are paired with younger students for Reading Partners, peer tutoring, and school community service projects. Student Council representatives have an opportunity to share and get feedback from members of the classes. The school guidance counselor provides homeroom teachers with activities that include role-playing, problem solving, and peer counseling to help students understand their emotions.

The Mission Statement for St. Charles Borromeo School states, in part, that "we strive for excellence in promoting the spiritual, intellectual, emotional, physical and cultural development of our students." For middle school students, that goal can sometimes be elusive, but I believe it is attainable.

Dual Roles

STELLA LAUERMAN
Assistant Principal
Madonna Del Sasso School
Salinas, CA

In my dual role as assistant principal and development director people sometimes ask me, "How can you do both jobs at once?" From my perspective, however, one position does not "conflict" or "interfere" with the other. *Everything* I do pertains to "institutional development," since "development" does not mean merely "fund raising," but rather advancement of the school in all its facets. One of my most important tasks as assistant principal is to help our principal communicate a clear understanding of our mission and ministry to all our constituencies. If we do not have a focused vision of our purpose, then the ten thousand and one details (in a day!) of school administration are for naught.

Ask any parent the question: "What is the most important thing in the world to you?" and the vast majority will respond, "Our children!" And rightly so — our children represent our life, our hopes and the future of our immediate families, our Church and our society at large. Madonna del Sasso Parish School creates a safe, nurturing environment where students can experience a maturing relationship with God, themselves, and others. Our Mission Statement clearly reflects this commitment: ". . . to motivate, instruct and nurture children in the beliefs, practices and values of the Catholic community integrated with the highest standards of academic excellence."

Probably the single most important element of a successful school, and, in turn, its development program, is a fundamental sense of *belonging*. If people feel they have been invited to be an integral part of the school family, whatever their relationship to it, then the "fund raising" eventually falls into place. Sparked by this essential personal connection, the school's direct constituencies are more than willing to support every aspect of the school's continued growth.

The effective dissemination of our mission to the community at large also encourages local businesses to recognize the value of investing in the academic and moral formation of our children for the future of our community.

Communication, both internal and external, is critical to building and fortifying the intangible fabric of a school's community. It is easy to fall into the trap of assuming that the parents and those close to the school automatically know the details of "what's going on" by osmosis. A clear and consistent invitation to be intimately and wholly involved in school life is the most important mechanism to foster the all-important sense of ownership. The school newsletter, web site and commercial media help to meet that need, both within the nucleus of the school family and the greater community. However, our greatest and probably the most effective medium of spreading our message, and by extension the Gospel message, is word of mouth. Once again, a personal connection, a heartfelt recommendation based on firsthand experience, has a far greater impact than any form of written communication.

Over the last three years, we have worked to create a Comprehensive Development Plan (CDP). This is a long range "blueprint" to streamline and consolidate our fund raising, in an effort to get away from the "nickel and dime" mentality that has characterized Catholic school fund raising, especially at the elementary level. The CDP serves as a resource document that provides everyone involved in the development process with a clear understanding of the components of the program and guides those involved in the development process in attaining development goals for the year.

We have undergone some major "paradigm shifts" in the last year relating to our school organization, in keeping with Dr. Gatta's admonition to "challenge all assumptions." Our Parents Club's original mission was to serve as a parent involvement group and to raise funds. We have taken the Parents' Club out of the fund raising business altogether and changed its focus to total dedication to community building activities. We even changed the name to the Home and School Association to underscore this change of emphasis and to highlight the connection between *home* and *school*.

The traditional offices have also been changed to reflect current roles and responsibilities rather than obsolete functions. We have cut out the "little" fund-raisers: the candy bar sales, bake sales and countless other schemes that cost the parents more, in time, effort, irritation, and calories, than they brought in. Rather, we are focusing on two major events, one sponsored solely by the school and the other in conjunction with the parish, again to build community and to utilize our resources, most importantly the human ones, effectively. We have also updated our Strategic Plan, which serves as a parallel document to the CDP to chart our course for the next few years.

The other significant elements of the CDP include the Annual Fund Plan, endowment and planned giving, and capital project fund raising. The purposes of the Annual Fund are congruent with our goal of promoting our mission and ministry. They include the education of alumni, friends, families and civic community of our area as to the vision, mission, goals and needs of our school as well as the invitation to participate and support the mission which will broaden that base of support. Endowment and planned giving are areas of the CDP that are still incipient for us; they will come into play as our development plan matures. The capital project of a gymnasium and other major improvements are also in the planning stages.

Enrollment management is not an issue for us. On the contrary, our reputation in the community is an excellent one, and issues relating to enrollment involve excess demand rather than a lack of potential applicants. However, complacency is a danger we must guard against. One of the tasks of the Development Committee is to study local demographic trends so that we will be conscious of changes in the community which may impact future enrollment.

Ultimately, the greatest measure of our development program and our overall success is the outstanding education that we are providing for our children. The children are happy and well-adjusted, their parents are pleased with the children's academic progress and the nurturing environment we provide for them, and the faculty and staff is a cohesive and dedicated group committed to fostering Catholic values within a rigorous curriculum. In short, Madonna del Sasso School is a great place to be, and we thank God every day for the many blessings He has bestowed upon us.

Growth for a Better You

CAROLYN LEVET
Assistant Principal
Visitation of Our Lady School
Marrero, LA

As an intrinsic part of Visitation of Our Lady School, our mission is to integrate the teachings of the Catholic Church with academic principles in developing each unique child. In our efforts to develop the whole child, we provide a strong basic curriculum along with spiritual and moral nurturing which will give our students the basis to go forth as faith-filled young adults. The mission of our school is the foundation upon which our programs are based. Therefore, it is impossible to separate the school's mission when designing or discussing students, programs, or faculty at Visitation of Our Lady.

For many years our school maintained a very stable faculty with a low teacher turnover rate. A traditional teacher evaluation program which centered on classroom observations was the method used for assessment. With the hiring of new teachers, we began to see the need to redesign our teacher evaluation process. Out of this concern, grew the need for a more comprehensive and self-reflective program to benefit the entire faculty. The goal was to foster improvement and development for both novice and veteran teachers. With teacher input and feedback, the idea of a self-reflective teaching portfolio was developed.

Collaborative decision making, steeped in trust, communication and openness is an integral part of our culture and mission; therefore input from the faculty was essential. A team consisting of administration and faculty members began designing a self-assessment portfolio that would promote growth and improvement. Although a portfolio is not a substitute for classroom observations, it can be a valuable extension for cultivating outstanding teaching and learning. The teacher evaluation portfolio is designed to empower teachers so they can evaluate themselves as professionals. The self evaluation is an evolving process. It begins with the start of school in August and continues throughout the year. Yearly, during contract signing, teachers share their portfolio with the principal. The information compiled is used to discuss the individual's professional growth, progress, and improvement.

The portfolio is divided into four sections: evidence from self, evidence from others, professional development, and weekly journal entries.

Evidence from Self: This self-evaluation section helps a teacher to focus on his/her feelings and ideas about teaching as well as reflecting on areas that need strengthening. The first part of this section asks the educator to read the school philosophy and then write his or her own philosophy of education. Although a bit daunting at first, it forces one to reflect on ideas, attitudes, and the basic perceptions one brings to teaching including the aim and purpose of education. This is a dated entry because one's philosophy is often evolving and changing with the benefit of experience. The second area of this section consists of several specific, self-evaluative questions. Some sample questions include: "What makes me a good teacher?", "How can I become a better teacher?", "What can I do to make Visitation a better school?", "What new teaching method would I like to learn more about?", "List three professional and personal goals for the school year." The last entry in the section is a written description of the teacher's best lesson. The lesson should be one that the teacher is most proud of and best defines his/her teaching style. Concrete evidence such as handouts, pictures, and tests should be included along with the description of the lesson.

Evidence from Others: This section demonstrates how others view one's teaching. Parent and student surveys are encouraged and included in the section. Sample surveys geared to various grade levels are included, or the teacher may design his/her own survey. All teachers are required to distribute, collect, and critically reflect on survey feedback. Also included in this section are samples of students' work as well as a reflection of the students' standardized test scores. Each year after scores are received, the faculty attends an inservice to analyze and discuss the results. Students' strengths and weaknesses are highlighted. Teachers use this information to set goals geared specifically at improving their instruction in low scoring areas.

Professional Development: In this section, teachers include professional development activities in which they have participated such as workshops or classes. Also, included are books and/or research completed on teaching and learning, and articles from professional journals or magazines. Monthly, each teacher is required to summarize an article and share it with other members of the faculty. In addition to the brief summaries of the article, the teacher also comments on how the topic is relevant to his/her teaching area. These professional reading and summations have widely broadened the knowledge and expertise of our faculty. New teaching methods and programs have materialized as a direct result of this component of the portfolio.

Weekly Journal Section: This final section was included for the teacher to reflect weekly on what is happening in their classroom. The following thoughts can be used to help teachers reflect on their weekly progress. "List one thing that really went well this week." "Is there any thing I will do differently in the future?" "Are there any relationships I need to work on?" "Is there anything in my personal life that is affecting my teaching?" "Did I do my best this week?" "List a goal for the upcoming week."

This self-assessment portfolio has been a powerful tool in the teacher evaluation process, and a great benefit to our teachers. Through reflection, teachers try to understand their actions and at times contemplate alternative solutions. This helps to enable a teacher to refine his/her approach and improve for future experiences. The teaching portfolio and self reflection process has led to growth and improvement for our teachers. Looking inward and honestly reflecting on one's own performance is often challenging and difficult. The ability to accomplish this is believed by some to be the mark of a true professional.

Science Fairs: A Valuable Tool in Mission Realization

SUE LONG
Assistant Principal
Our Lady of the Assumption School
San Bernardino, CA

During the summer of 2001, I had the opportunity to participate in the NCEA Assistant Principals Academy held in Washington, D.C. My colleagues and I arrived from all over the country, bringing with us our own unique experiences and accomplishments. One fact was immediately apparent; there is absolutely no such thing as a one-size-fits-all job description for an assistant principal. Our areas of expertise and responsibilities were as diverse as the states and dioceses from which we came. Yet, as different as we were, it was quite clear that for each of us, the service we provided for our students was driven by our individual school's mission statement.

As is the case with most Catholic school mission statements, the mission statement of my school, Our Lady of the Assumption, states our dedication to the Good News of Christ and to our focus on the spiritual, moral, physical, and academic growth of each student. We also seek to foster respect and compassion for all of God's creation. Worthy goals all, but how to put them into motion? One tool I have used over the years is the annual Science Fair.

PURPOSE:

The purpose of a science fair is to allow all students the opportunity to familiarize themselves with the scientific method. This is a step-by-step approach to problem solving which is valuable across the disciplines. It is a useful tool for students as they pursue academics, and is equally important as a life skill. Science fairs encourage students to develop analytical and process skills, while at the same time enhancing critical thinking. Science fairs also provide students with an investigative environment in which to pursue their curiosity and a forum to refine communication skills through the sharing of student findings. In addition, group projects promote cooperative learning and social interaction. Many desirable objectives can be attained through the employment of this single educational vehicle. What a deal!

While each school decides its own science fair schedule, some aspects are common to all schools. A successful science fair requires planning and involvement by the school community. Teachers prepare their students using models and examples; coordinators set due dates, arrange for display areas, and establish judging criteria if awards are to be given; parents and community volunteers serve as judges and spectators. Overall, science fairs are excellent forums for community interaction.

TEACHER RESPONSIBILITIES:

Science fairs are fun! Encourage students to explore their curiosity; have them pick something that interests them, then work within the guidelines the teacher determines. These will vary with each grade. Texts generally outline variations of the scientific method, giving examples of the steps involved. Examples of level appropriate projects follow:

- **K - 3:** Students at the primary level may choose to display collections; i.e. rocks from areas they have visited, pictures of animals they have identified, categorizations of leaves from the neighborhood, etc. Models illustrating basic science concepts or subject areas might also be displayed. These could include, for example, how a lever works, or a model of the inner earth or solar system. It is at this level that students are introduced to the scientific method, which can be modified to age-appropriate levels.

- **4 - 6:** Students at the intermediate level should have projects which illustrate further development and understanding of the scientific method. For example, explorations of which kinds of materials conduct heat or electricity best, what are the best insulators, which soil conditions promote growth for particular plants, etc. Models displayed at this level should illustrate more complex scientific principles, such as the workings of a motor, the most effective hazard signs, and so on.

- **7 - 8:** At this level, students should display a detailed project based on all the steps of the scientific method (shown below). The project should include statement of a problem and a step-by-step approach to solving this problem. In addition, a research paper and/or journal should accompany the experiment which the student is presenting. This paper explains the student's work, following scientific method guidelines.

THE SCIENTIFIC METHOD:

1) **Observation:** What is something the student would like to find out? A project is based on an idea students get from observing the world around them.

2) **Purpose:** Also known as problem, this is usually stated as a question. Why does the student's observation happen? What would happen if a variable was altered in some way?

3) **Research:** The purpose of the experiment drives the background research. This includes what is already known about

the subject under study, work by famous scientists and/or discoveries in the field, etc. The teacher may set the guidelines as to the amount and type of information necessary, the number of required sources, and so on.

4) **Hypothesis:** This is stated as a sentence, i.e., "Carbon dioxide is heavier than air." The hypothesis is an educated guess based on the student's observations and research.

5) **Procedure:** The steps of the experiment are explained here. Instructors stress the necessity of controls, changing one variable at a time, etc. The procedure includes the materials used, and the method by which the student came to his or her results.

6) **Experiment:** This is what the student actually did. The experiment is the student's process of gathering the information which confirms or negates the hypothesis. It is through the experiment that the student gains data.

7) **Results:** The data is gained from the experiment. This information can be displayed in an appropriate manner, such as charts, graphs, tables, etc.

8) **Conclusion:** This is an analysis of the results, and a statement of what the experiment has illustrated. Was the hypothesis correct? What other questions has the experiment led the student to ask? In other words, what's next?

Teachers should stress that an essential aspect of any experiment is that it is reproducible. Therefore, communication of the method followed, analysis of results, and a record of all actions taken which relate to the science project is a necessity. This record is the log, or journal, which accompanies the student's physical display. Again, teachers set the parameters and communicate expectations to the students through models, lectures, etc.

COORDINATOR RESPONSIBILITIES:

Coordinators are responsible for the "nuts and bolts" of the fair. They work with teachers to set dates for projects displayed to the rest of the school and the public. If judges are to be used, coordinators contact volunteers for dates and times of project viewing. As a rule, it is a good idea to allow judges privacy while they are evaluating projects. Then, once they have finished, coordinators should collect their scores, tally them, and then turn the scores over to individual teachers for further evaluation and assessment. Again, this is a school-by-school decision; what is effective for one school may not be for another. However, it should be determined in advance whether or not teachers will allow the raw judging scores to be viewed by students.

Science fair projects represent a lot of work by students and their families. For this reason, recognition in the form of a certificate, extra recess, etc., is recommended for all participants. Coordinators work with teachers to accomplish this. In addition, judges should receive thank you notes for donating time and talent. As previously stated, judges are not a necessity, but if participation in the state or regional science fairs is a goal, placement is usually determined through school competition.

PARENT/COMMUNITY RESPONSIBILITIES:

Since science fair projects are so time-intensive, parental involvement is a necessity. Teachers need to convey this to parents at the very beginning of the science fair process. This allows parents the opportunity to incorporate project requirements, i.e. taking their child to the library, purchasing materials, etc., into their time schedules. In addition, since much of the project work is completed at home, parent-teacher communication is very effective in keeping students on track.

Community involvement is highly desirable in science fairs. Coordinators may draw on community members as judges. Also, the display of student work makes a very interesting tour, and is an excellent way to highlight school accomplishments.

Student participation in science fairs is very rewarding for the entire school community. Not only are individual students actively involved in problem-solving, self-expression, and communication, they also benefit from the work of their peers, as do the student's families and friends who come to view the science projects. Overall, science fairs are effective community-builders as well as educational tools.

A Plan for Local Inservice: Maximizing the Potential of Students Through Teacher Education

Maureen Marsteller
Assistant Principal
St. Louis de Marillac School
Pittsburgh, PA

St. Louise de Marillac School espouses a philosophy that includes the following words, "...to provide the students with the knowledge, skills, and attitudes that are necessary to achieve a high degree of success in life, maximizing their potential." To work toward the fulfillment of this mission, it is my responsibility to develop inservice presentations for the faculty. Technology, society, and core material, to mention a few critical areas, have all changed to some extent. If we are to maximize student potential, then we have to make sure that we have the best, most informed teachers to do the job. Teacher development is an essential component of school improvement.

In addition to our desire to live our philosophy, our inservice activities are also tied directly into the state of Pennsylvania's mandate that each teacher completes 180 hours of continuing professional education, or any combination of collegiate studies, continuing professional education courses or learning experiences equivalent to one hundred eighty hours every five years (Act 48 of 1999). At the end of each presentation, Performance-based Assessment/Continuing Professional Education Experience Evaluation Forms are distributed, collected, tallied, and sent to the Diocese of Pittsburgh. As an approved provider of continuing education, the Diocese can submit fifteen hours of local (school-based) inservice for each teacher. The number of hours submitted depends on the number of hours provided through the local school. Therefore, it is to each school's advantage to develop an inservice program that includes at least fifteen hours of instruction and meets the educational requirements of the state of Pennsylvania.

Prior to becoming an approved provider, the Diocese of Pittsburgh had to have a professional education plan approved by the Pennsylvania Department of Education. In its proposal, the Diocese identified seven goal areas as targets of its educational plan. They are: Differentiated Instruction; Technology; Continuous Improvement of the Core Curriculum; Special Needs of Learners; Leadership/Administration; Teacher Mentoring; and, Area(s) of Assignment and/or Certification. When planning different inservice opportunities, it was necessary to ensure that the topic under consideration fell into one of the goal areas.

As an administrator, it was not hard to pinpoint critical areas of inservice need. Observation, teacher discussion, and administrative need are just a few of the ways in which ideas for inservice can be garnered. Observation is defined as recognition of reoccurring problems that are common to many grade levels. By circulating throughout the building, and being aware of problems that occur, it is often easy to see when a general topic is germane to the wide range of ages taught in the school. Teacher discussion is defined as conversations, formal or informal, that take place between the faculty and administration. Teachers may feel the need to be briefed on new ideas or techniques and may appreciate being part of the inservice decision-making process. Administrative decision comes into play when items such as legal responsibility, curriculum changes or mandated subjects are topics that must be presented.

This year, our inservice opportunities will focus on five areas of identified need:

- grieving children (special needs of learners),
- classroom management with a focus on student discipline (differentiated instruction),
- recognition of adolescents in crisis (special needs of learners),
- classroom management of students with Attention Deficit Disorder (special needs of learners), and
- managing change, both personal and classroom (continuous improvement of core curriculum).

Each of these topics alone could take days to develop and discuss. For our purposes, it was in keeping with our philosophy to present an overview of information on a variety of topics. If the need arises to more fully develop a topic, it will be done at a later date. This does limit the amount of time available for each topic and, therefore, the format used to present the information may change according to time limitations. However, in each instance, a basic review of research will be presented along with handouts that give specific references to other sources of information pertaining to the topic discussed. Guest presenters, large and small group activities, as well as videos will serve to enhance the presentations when time permits. A brief summary of each inservice follows.

The first activity will center on one agency available for helping grieving children. Over the years we've had a number of school parents die and have often felt inadequate in our ability to help the child. Recently the administration was made aware of a facility in Pittsburgh that helps children and families deal with the loss of a loved one. It was felt that this would be an excellent opportunity to assist our faculty in helping a child. The faculty will report to The Caring Center where they will be given a presentation of the role of the Center in the community, engage in a question and answer session, and then will tour the facility.

Our second inservice will deal with student discipline and will include the idea of classroom management designed to prevent problems. Time is severely limited due to the fact that this will be part of a regular faculty meeting. A review of current research will be presented orally and visually with a hard copy distributed after the presentation. This hard copy will also include references to further information available. A large group question/answer session will precede a small group role-playing activity. Sharing of disciplinary techniques will also highlight the session.

The presentation of "Adolescents in Crisis" will include a review of research enhanced by a video entitled, "Adolescents in Crisis: Recognition and Intervention." Discussion will follow.

Attention Deficit Disorder is always a subject of concern, and is a topic that has been addressed previously in more informal settings. So this session will be a follow up on what teachers already know. Recent research will be presented followed by a video entitled, "Classroom Management of the Child with Attention Deficit Disorder."

Our final inservice opportunity will deal with the subject of change, both personal and in the educational setting. A packaged program is available from the publishers of the book, *Who Moved My Cheese?*. This will be utilized and then personalized with discussion opportunities that follow.

For many of the sessions, it is my responsibility to be both the designer and facilitator, roles that I truly enjoy. Each year will provide a new opportunity for me to educate the faculty in a way that is enjoyable and meaningful.

As stated earlier, I regard teacher improvement as the key to school improvement. I am honored to be in charge of such an important task.

Fostering Responsibility and Accountability: B.I.S.T.

JANE MAURER
*Assistant Principal
St. Peter Interparish School
Jefferson City, MO*

In the fall of 1999, the assistant principal was introduced to a discipline model—B.I.S.T.—a program that was proving to be effective in a neighboring public school. At the Ozanam Home of Kansas City, Missouri, the discipline model or B.I.S.T. (Behavior Intervention Support Team), as it is called, seemed to us to have two major components, GRACE and Accountability, to assist in addressing "What Kids Need" to foster self-discipline, personal responsibility, and accountability. This disciplinary model appeared to be one that would help us carry out the philosophy of St. Peter Interparish School: "to provide a quality education rich in Catholic identity" and to "develop self-discipline, personal responsibility, and accountability" in our students.

After observing B.I.S.T. in a school setting and participating in a discussion of the model, a volunteer team of ten staff members, consisting of the assistant principal, school counselor, teachers, and aides, were sent to a five-day summer training program in the rationale and implementation of the B.I.S.T. model. The school B.I.S.T. Team then presented it to the entire school staff for implementation in the fall of 2000. Minor changes to the model were made to adapt it to our setting and students' needs within the first year. Additional training for the entire staff was given at the end of the school year to address problems and questions that came up during the year and to further instill the procedures. The staff, realizing need for continuing education in developing the procedures of this model, requested additional inservicing during the school term.

The B.I.S.T. model calls for "GRACE"—the unconditional support educators provide students in saying: "I accept: 1) You; 2) Your problems; 3) It is a part of a problem in my life; 4) Your need." That means to be unconditionally supportive in helping students to stay out of trouble, to be okay and safe. "Accountability—on the part of the student, calls for responsibility from the student in acknowledging: "1) I did it; 2) I'm sorry; 3) It is a part of a problem in my life; 4) I accept consequences; 5) I accept and need help."

When a student disrupts a class, the teacher addresses the student with a question such as "Can you be safe where you are and (mention the desired behavior)? If the disruption continues, the student is directed to the classroom "safe seat," an area in the classroom where the student can continue to work on or listen to the instruction. Disruptive students who are not safe, i.e., who continue to cause disruption in the classroom "safe seat," are sent to a prearranged "Focus Room" (The B.I.S.T. term for the "Focus Room" is the "Buddy Room." We made this name change so as to not confuse it with another program in the school). The student reporting to a "Focus Room" is shown to an out of the way area to complete a "Think Sheet" and to do assigned work.

The 'Think Sheet" helps the student address all five steps of "Accountability." This also provides a cool-down period for the student and allows the referring teacher to continue the lesson without disruption as well as to help deescalate a situation that could cause "tempers to fly." The student then makes an appointment to process with the adult (the playground supervisor, classroom teacher, or administrator directly involved with the disruptive incident) to work out a plan to address the problem. Changes begin to occur for the student when he or she works through the "Think Sheet" and through processing with the adult and works out a plan to address steps 3-5 in "Accountability." It is important to note that step 3, "accepting consequences," is meant to help the student to begin implementing change. Consequences are not to be punitive. It is during the processing with the referring teacher that it is determined whether or not a student is ready to return to the classroom or playground. Students who are sent to the "Focus Room" usually remain there until the end of the class period. The times vary according to grade level and the time of the disruption. A referring teacher may request that a student remain in the "Focus Room" for another period, depending on the circumstances and the readiness of the student to return to the classroom. The referring adult may call or send home a note to simply inform parents of the incident. This notification is made to keep parents informed and to keep communications open between home and school.

Students who cause disruption in a "Focus Room" or fight on the playground are sent to an administrator. Parents are called when this happens. It has been our experience that parents have been very appreciative of this simple notification which informs them of the plan of action their child has worked out to correct the inappropriate behavior.

Students quickly learn the procedures set down in the model and the terminology that is used. Students have also learned to express to the supervising adult: "I am not okay here. May I sit in the 'safe seat' or other location?" One junior high student toward the end of the school year was having difficulty managing behavior during the transition periods and asked the homeroom teacher and assistant principal if it would be okay to spend those times in the assistant principal's office closely located to the junior high classrooms. Accommodations were made and the student said that he felt this was a good plan for him in order to stay out of trouble.

Habitual disruption by a student indicates that more time

is needed to work through their problems and to develop a plan. After working with the model for a year, the staff decided to add the next phase set up in the B.I.S.T. model, the "Recovery Room." The "Recovery Room" consists of a day or more, as needed, during which the disruptive student takes all classes, breaks, and lunch with a substitute teacher so that classes may be taught without disruption and learning can take place. The goal of the "Recovery Room" is to help the disruptive student to do a better job of creating a plan that will help him or her to have a better day in the regular classroom. Parents or guardians are required to pay the going rate per day for the substitute for the day or days a student needs to be in the "Recovery Room."

Another component of the B.I.S.T. model is "Triage." Triage is a way to provide early intervention for unpredictable children to prevent acting out. Triage assists the child in establishing responsibility for the outcome of their day and to develop relationships with adults. "Triage" is an area that we hope to develop as we progress in the use of this model of assisting students in becoming more self-disciplined, responsible, and accountable.

>   For more information contact:
>   Ozanam Home
>   Behavioral Intervention Support Team
>   421 E. 137th Street
>   Kansas City, MO 64165
>   816-508-3652

STOP: Moral Decision-Making in the Upper Elementary Grades

AMY L. MEAD
Assistant Principal,
Our Lady of Mercy School
Baton Rouge, LA

Moral decision-making can be taught in the upper elementary grades. By demonstrating the four steps to the whole class, the teacher can help students refine their decision-making process while in small groups and then individually using situations that are meaningful to them.

The four steps are **S – T – O – P.**
   S – search for the facts
   T – think of other alternatives
   O – get the opinions of others
   P – pray

Each situation begins with a search for the facts. Sometimes missing pieces of information greatly affect decisions that have to be made. After the facts have been found, alternative solutions are suggested. It is important for the teacher to write down every alternative suggested. This leads to the third step. Find out what the group's opinions are for each alternative. After discussion, decide which alternative would be most acceptable. The final step is to pray. Have the group compose a prayer for the spiritual support of their decision.

EXAMPLE WORKSHEET:

Ima Student received a report card on Monday. Every subject went down one letter grade:

Reading – D   English – C-   Social Studies – F
Math – D   Science – F   Religion – D

Ima hid the report card until Friday morning when her parents were in a rush and had to sign it quickly.

PROBLEM: Ima hid report card from parents

S   -the grades were all lower
-Ima hid report card from parents
-Ima did not want parents to see it

T   -explain to parents what happened during the grading period
-don't show the report card to them the next time
-make-up a story about the bad grades

O   -this is a good alternative – Ima should own up to the bad grades
-this is not good – Ima will be in more trouble next time
-this is not good – lying will not help Ima's situation

P   Dear God, help me make good decisions. When I have not done my best, help me to be honest about the problems I may be having. I know my parents care for me and want me to do my best. Sometimes it is hard to do that when I don't understand something. I promise to ask for help.

When the group has completed the problem worksheet and understands the steps, assign a new problem to small groups. There are good examples from comic strips in the newspaper that address common problems students have in their lives. Other small group problems could be:

The Doctor and the Mid-Air Crisis

Dear Ann Landers:

I was on a plane between San Francisco and Chicago recently. The gentlemen seated next to me was pleasant and friendly. Shortly after take-off we began to chat, and I learned he was a physician.

An hour into the flight, there seemed to be some commotion in the back section of the plane. Several flight attendants hurried anxiously in that direction.

After a few moments the captain's voice was heard: "Is there a physician aboard? Please put on your call button. We have a sick passenger who needs attention."

The man seated next to me continued to read his magazine as if he hadn't heard a thing. I waited a few moments and finally asked, "Did you hear the captain's announcement?" The doctor replied, "Yes, but I choose not to get involved. Two years ago a cardiologist friend of mine was sued ... for being a Good Samaritan. The woman he pulled out of the wreckage on a highway died, and her family really took him to the cleaners."

My curiosity finally got the better of me. I went back to see what was going on and saw two rather young men assisting the patient. I learned they were medical students. An ambulance met the plane, and I have no idea what happened after that.

When I said adios to my seatmate, I confess I had lost a lot of respect for him. What are your views on this subject?

—Clouded Vision

Lifeboat Morals

A movie entitled *Abandon Ship* depicts in a general way a famous legal case in American law, *U.S. v. Holmes,* 26 Fed. Cases 360 (1842). It tells the story of a ship's captain who decided to sacrifice some lives on a life raft. He did so in the face of severe criticism by some of the passengers and at a personal risk to his own life.

The lifeboat could hold at its maximum only 14 people; there were 26 who survived the shipwreck. The situation became desperate when a severe storm arose. There was no immediate hope of rescue; on the contrary, it looked as if help would come only after a number of days or not at all.

His decision in the face of severe protest was to put some of the survivors over the side. They were outfitted with life jackets. His criterion for choosing was the "survival of the fittest." He anticipated that there would be a long row to land, a journey of maybe several weeks.

Thus, he chose those who had to leave the boat: a man who had inhaled the fumes of fuel oil; an elderly man and his wife, too weak to row the long haul to the coast; a weakened sailor who had not yet reached adulthood; and other people he judged weak and infirm. The others in the lifeboat refused to help put the victims over the sides of the boat except at gunpoint.

Soon after he put them overboard, the storm ended. Unexpectedly, the lifeboat and its occupants were rescued the next day. All aboard refused to accept responsibility for the captain's actions.

The Heinz Dilemma

The following philosophical dilemma was posed to individuals by Lawrence Kohlberg and his colleagues in their research on moral decision-making. You are asked to consider the following situation:

> A woman is dying of cancer. A new drug that could save her life has been discovered by the local druggist. The druggist, who has not invested much in the drug, sells it for $2,000 – about ten times what it cost him to make the drug. Heinz, the sick woman's husband, tries to borrow the money from friends, but he can raise only $1,000. He approaches the druggist, asking him to sell the drug for half the price or let him, the husband, repay the rest at a later time. The druggist refuses. The husband, in desperation, breaks into the store and steals the drug.

When the small group problems have been discussed, choose a problem for each student to decide individually. Have each student completes a STOP worksheet.

Safety in Our School

MONICA MOSS
Assistant Principal
Immaculate Heart of Mary School
Indianapolis, IN

Our mission statement at Immaculate Heart of Mary School says, "We are committed to the spirit, academic, social and emotional growth of each child." We will not be able to meet these needs if the safety of the child is not put as priority. I head a new committee in our school: the Safety Committee, started for the families of Immaculate Heart of Mary School.

The committee is made up of seven members and is comprised of parents new to the school, seasoned parents, the school social worker, the school maintenance supervisor and myself. The committee has been larger at times but we have felt more progress was made with a smaller number of people. All members are important pieces in making up the committee. The administration is the link to the staff to relay information. As head of the committee I set up the meeting agenda which is sent to each member one week before the meeting. The maintenance person is important because he/she implements the physical changes necessary to the school building. The social worker is up to date on the needs of our children in various ways (e.g., guns and gangs). New parents bring fresh ideas and are willing to do thing in new ways. Seasoned parents remind us of what has been successful or unsuccessful in the past. *Our goal is to work together as a group to provide a safer environment for our children at school.*

The Safety Committee is active throughout the year. Meetings are held monthly in a building adjacent to the school. By having the meetings outside of the school building, it has decreased interruptions.

This past year the committee worked in a number of areas to make our school a safer place. The committee has taken on the responsibility of creating and circulating an emergency phone tree for the school. We released information to the teachers and posted information by each telephone about bomb threats. A committee member made professional floor plans of our school and made sure copies were given to the fire department and to the sheriff. We ordered new crosswalk signs for our school intersections. The committee decided how to handle hostage or intruder situations and the administration reviewed the lock down procedures with the staff. We also reviewed the schools' dismissal policy and will implement the changes decided by the committee in the fall. The committee took the responsibility for distributing and summarizing parent surveys. We updated and distributed emergency handbooks. The committee was responsible for the individual notes sent to families concerning safety issues. We kept staff up to date on decisions made by the committee. Each member took responsibility for his or her assignments for the committee before the next meeting.

Some changes in the committee we are looking to make in the fall will be to have a rotating person to take notes, type them and distribute them to committee members. We will have the goal of keeping our meeting to the length of one hour and a half. We will set meeting dates at the previous meeting when other members are present to check their calendars.

In closing, I feel that our new committee has been a success. The subtle changes will happen over time to help our committee to serve our school in its' highest capacity. Again, our goal is very simply to provide a safer environment for our children. If you have any questions about our safety committee, please do not hesitate to contact me.

A.P.T. to Succeed

MARY JEAN QUILL
Assistant Principal
St. Elizabeth Elementary School
Wilmington, DE

Adolescence is a critical time in human development. In today's confusing and ever- changing world, adolescents need more guidance, time, and attention to be prepared to meet the challenges of adulthood. St. Elizabeth Elementary School is committed to educating the mind, body, and spirit of her students by assisting parents in their primary right and responsibility to form and educate their children into mature witnesses of Christ. The faculty strives to integrate values and beliefs throughout all academic and social areas. As a reflection of the school's mission and philosophy and to assist adolescents cope with challenges, a structured advisory program, "A.P.T" has been implemented for the eighth graders. A.P.T stands for Adolescents, Parents, and Teachers. Through the program, parents and teachers work together to assist the students in learning life skills needed to succeed in today's world. It is apt, suitable, and fitting that adolescents, parents and teachers work together for success.

To begin each school year, the eighth graders are divided into small groups. The size and number of groups can easily be adapted for any school. It is suggested that the advisors from the groups rather than the students create an environment in which students will have the opportunity to get to know a variety of students on a deeper level as the year progresses. Once the groups are formed, a faculty member serves as advisor to a group. In addition to facilitating the formal weekly advisory sessions, each moderator tracks his or her advisees throughout the year, meeting with students individually to discuss academic or behavioral progress and to provide opportunities to speak privately on any issue the students wish to discuss. At all times, students are encouraged to seek guidance through prayer and from parents, teachers, and other trusted adults whenever needed. The interaction both in formal advisory sessions and informal meetings enables students and teachers to create stronger bonds in a setting outside the classroom. A relationship of trust between students and teachers is established so the adolescents know there is always someone there for help and support.

A formal advisory book is created by the advisory team and used each school year. The book contains weekly lessons which are grouped into theme units. Sample units include: goal setting, moral decision making, substance abuse, preparing for high school, study skills, interpersonal management, and prayer. At the conclusion of each unit an open forum is scheduled at which time the students chose their own topics for discussion. Past topics have included stress reduction, coping with peer pressure, tolerance, school violence, and eating disorders. The program is flexible enough to allow for an open forum at any time to accommodate issues and concerns as they arise. In keeping with the Benedictine tradition of "Ora et Labora" (Prayer and Work) on which the school is based, each session begins with prayer or reflection. The success of each session depends on the students' willingness to share with and listen to each other. At the conclusion of each session is a brief explanation to parents regarding the topic discussed and space for the parents to sign. This enables parents to be kept informed and provides the opportunity to strengthen dialogue between the students and their parents. Any school implementing an advisory program can easily choose topics most pertinent for the needs of its own students.

At the end of the school year, a formal evaluation is completed by parents, students and advisors to assess the strengths and weaknesses of the program and to make changes as needed. The assessment process is critical to determine the effectiveness and direction of the program and to keep it timely and meaningful for all involved. A sampling of responses is included here.

Parent Responses
- "I feel it does help the children make the right moral decisions."
- "It provided the opportunity to discuss issues that we may not have otherwise discussed."
- "My child finds it easier to discuss difficult issues and concerns with me."

Student Responses
- "I am able to talk to my parents now and they know where I am coming from so they understand me."
- "The program has helped me feel more comfortable and confident in choosing the right decisions."
- "They should have this program in high school."

Teacher Responses
- "It is wonderful seeing the students gain a greater appreciation for each other as they have the opportunity to share their ideas, concerns, and opinions."
- "I truly enjoy the students learning more about me as I learn more about them in a setting outside the classroom."
- "The bonds which form among the students in the advisory group as the year progresses remind the students they are not alone in their journey through life. Parents, teachers, peers, and their faith are there to help them succeed physically, emotionally, and spiritually."

In addition to formal evaluation, success is measured through shared laughter, support in times of sorrow, concern for each other's health and well-being, and courage demonstrated by choosing what is right but not necessarily popular.

> "Prefer nothing to Christ, and may Christ bring us all together to everlasting life."
> ~*The Rule of St. Benedict*

From the founding of St. Elizabeth Elementary School in 1908, the Benedictine Sisters, teachers, and support staff have worked to impress this desire into the hearts of all students. Through participation in the A.P.T. program, it is the advisors' fervent desire that our eighth grade graduates keep Christ in their hearts and minds as they travel through life and that they will draw upon the skills and values needed to succeed as ambassadors of Christ.

School Masses

CAROLYN WILDE
Assistant Principal
Our Lady of Lourdes Catholic School
Salt Lake City, UT

Our mission statement says that: *Our Lady of Lourdes Catholic School exists to create a Catholic, Christian learning environment in which students can grow in academic knowledge and the realization of God working in their lives.* This statement compels us to keep searching for ways to integrate our Catholic traditions into our classroom settings. My principal wanted to improve the students' celebration of our school liturgies. This became my project as Assistant Principal and full time kindergarten teacher. In the past, one teacher put a Mass together and gave it to a classroom teacher. That teacher was then responsible for organizing her class to perform that Mass. We wanted to change that. Our objectives were to form some traditions as to how our Masses were planned, to make the experience of the liturgy more meaningful to our children, to involve each student in a leadership role, and to make our school Mass a culminating activity of classroom study.

How I got started

I knew that once school started my teaching responsibilities would fill my time, so I spent some summer time researching different saints' lives. I had decided that choosing one saint to study each month would be a good starting point and could involve the whole school. So, using saints' lives and the Internet, I found saints whose lives highlighted different characteristics we could all study and incorporate in our prayer life, and whose feast days correlated with our school schedule. I chose:

- September: Opening of School
- October: St Francis of Assisi - love of animals and the environment
- November: All Saints Day - following Christ
- December: Blessed Mother Mary - saying yes to God
- January: St Elizabeth Ann Seton - celebrating Catholic Schools
- February: St. Bernadette - celebrating our school
- March: St. Joseph - love of family
- April: St. Benedict the Moor - celebrating our diversity
- May: Graduation Mass
- June: End of School - sharing the Good News through the summer

How I did it

At our opening faculty meeting, we let every teacher choose a month to be responsible for Mass. We also discussed, as a faculty, some of the Mass procedures: where children sit, where and how we show reverence, how we move in the church, etc. Teachers took responsibility to put these procedures into practice. I promised teachers that I would give them some resource materials and activities to add to their lessons that correlated to the saint and topic for the month. Here is where my summer studies really came in handy. I requested that they use the materials so that when it came time for Mass, all students had been exposed to the Mass theme. I also gave these materials to our priest. He added comments and little assignments in his homily that students and teachers could discuss back in the classroom. Students took this seriously.

During the school year, I met with each teacher and class and we discussed the Mass. We were able to use the strengths and creativity of our students and teachers to make Masses reverent, yet unique to each class. We talked about the Mass order, tradition, leadership roles, songs, petition prayers, and readings. I really enjoyed this time and our discussions with each class. I was able to clear up some misconceptions and accentuate student involvement and participation. I asked the students to volunteer for different "jobs" during Mass: readers, processions, choir singers, dancers, and musicians. The classroom teacher and I matched the child to the job he/she wanted to do. I found asking children to write the job on a slip of paper not only saved time, but also made children responsible for their own choice. My influence on the selection of students for responsibilities determined that children of all abilities had important parts. Readings were separated into smaller parts, a candle or flowers were added to processions, rhythm instruments were used and introductions to readings or songs were added. All children had an important responsibility and often it was their first choice!

Each class was responsible for writing their own petitions. Our teachers were very creative at getting these written. Some worked as whole class; some had each student write a petition and the class decide which ones to use at Mass; some divided the class into groups and each group wrote a petition; some gave topics and the students came up with the way the petition was worded. I was always amazed with the ideas and concerns our children had for petitions.

I gave the music teacher the parts of the Mass music and asked her to teach that music to all classes. Each month, I also gave her different hymns to teach to all classes. In kindergarten, we used Mass music as our closing prayer on many days. With the help of the art teacher, we added artwork to the bulletin board outside the school office that matched the theme of the Mass. We all worked together to make our school Masses more meaningful.

Evaluation

Our school community was very pleased with our school Masses. Teachers liked having me help them with the Mass protocol. I was able to remove some of the dread that teachers felt in planning a Mass. Students liked being a part of the decision making and the responsibility that came from those decisions. Students from the other classes felt empathy for the class responsible for the Mass and because of that, they were focused and behavior improved dramatically. More parents attended their child's class Mass. Parishioners commented on the reverent behavior and participation of students. My principal was pleased with the way we celebrated Mass and the correlation between Mass and the classroom. The discussions and comments among students showed their pride in their prayer experiences. As Assistant Principal, I was able to work with and get to know each class. I used my planning times and lunch times to work with other classes so my primary responsibility, as kindergarten teacher, was not compromised. We have already decided to expand this next school year by incorporating our whole school activity to our Mass theme.

Our school family, working together, grew in their awareness of the Eucharist as a communal celebration of God's love in their lives. The other jobs I had as Assistant Principal paled in comparison to the mission of this undertaking.